To Family,

Love,

The Journey Home

The Journey Home

Leslie L. Dame
Editor: Barbara Hancock

Library of Congress Control Number: 2014903987

ISBN:	Hardcover	978-1-4931-8057-8
	Softcover	978-1-4931-8058-5
	Ebook	978-1-4931-8056-1

This book was printed in the United States of America.

Rev. date: 05/08/2014

To order additional copies of this book, contact:
Xlibris LLC
1-888-795-4274
www.Xlibris.com
Orders@Xlibris.com
606817

CONTENTS

11 Introduction

13 As A Child

A Weekend Morning Of Childhood....15
And Again, One Child's Saturday Morning....16

17 Staunch Lessons

Centre College Affair....19
Last Night....20
Leave Taking....21

23 Changes of Seasons In Pieces Of The City

City Night....25
Acorns In August....26
Autumn Sunday At The River....27
Winter Night....28
Winter Walk....29

31 The Trauma

Winter's Coming....33
Bleak Omens....34
Storms....35
Dad....36
Mom....37

39 In Expectation of Christmas Looking From Out of the Hospital Place

Winter's Promise....41
Awaiting....42
Advent Sunday Morning....43
Preparation....44
Christ Is Coming....45
Outside The Christmas Window....46

47 Psychosis
Confusion 49
Undetected Domination 50

51 Looking Out From Other Hospital Spaces
In Here 53
Hope 54
Today 55
Dark 56
Out 57

59 A Goodbye To Dad
Healing Hands of Old 61
New York 62
Our Doctor 65
This Christmas At Church, After Dad 67

69 The Mental Ward—Again
Monday, August 27, 2007 71
A Total Eclipse of the Moon
Monday, August 27, 2007 73
Full Eclipse Of The Moon
Tuesday In August 74
Following The Full Eclipse Of The Moon
Night Again 75

77 Thoughts of Worship
After The Service 79
Saint Mark's 80
The Church 81

83 Winter
Cold Winter's Morning 85
February Snow 86
Brisk Rest 87
Paltry The Day 88
Night Walk 89

91 Spring
Growing Up 93
Spring 94
Spring Day 95
Knowing 96

97 Mom, Dad and Me
I Wish I Had 99
A Man Of Healing 104
The Prayer Bench 105

DEDICATION

To
My Sister,
Elston Lee Dame,
Both
Kind and Thoughtful!
She Gave Me
The
Courage
To Do This.

INTRODUCTION

I became a resident of Louisville, Kentucky from Syracuse, New York near the age of one year. My father was leaving from medical school at Cornell University and residency in Syracuse to set up practice in Louisville. My mother had been born and—except for brief intervals, brought up here. This is also where my parents, through dear friends Joyce and Dave Landon, had met. My father was satisfied to be settling in Kentucky, where his mother had been born.

At the time my parents moved back to Louisville, I was the 2nd child, with a one-year-older sister, Lee, who has long been an important mentor to me. We rented a house down the street from my maternal grandparents—my grandmother was a big help to us as my grandfather was mostly off working.

Our family started out at St. Mark's Episcopal Church, where my parents had been married. After many years at other churches, I am once again a member of St. Mark's, as is my younger sister, Lisa, and her son—my intelligent and well-mannered nephew, Sam.

I switched congregations after going through a very bad time. I stopped many things, but mostly I think about how I stopped running—and that was not a good thing. I am trying to get back to it—all that good exercise outside.

Lisa has stayed steady with her exercise and some running—mostly indoors on her treadmill.

My youngest sibling, and only brother, Curt, attends St. Mark's when he gets to church and he works out daily.

One could note that we could keep each other in line in these two areas except that I've had such a rough go of it for a time; I have really 'fallen off' and need to get back going.

Curt is often the host for extended family gatherings. His house is in Oxmoor Woods and with all the improvements he's made, it's a wonderful place for these parties that often include many friends.

Clearly family is important to me. My older sister, Lee, still attends the church that was important to some family and both parents before they passed away—Calvary Episcopal on South Fourth Street. Generally, exercise is not important to her; however, she is quite definitely the family cook. She is also our document holder and record keeper.

Religion is very important; I pray every morning and after church I try to get to Cave Hill Cemetery, where my parents are buried. A 'prayer bench' anchors the family plot. I do spend time on this bench after church.

My reading, at present, includes my grandmother's letters to my father while he was in the service. There are quite a number of them. Lee was the one to preserve them and put them on the computer. His responses are not yet on the computer—I'll probably be the one to do that.

My other reading includes Madeleine L'Engle—suggested by Lee. She's serious about religion and a lover of animals as we've all been in my family. Emily Dickenson was also a gift from Lee to me at a young age. I believe the book was a Christmas gift.

Robert Frost was a must-read gained from experience and education. E.B. White was one of my father's reads so I picked him up. Another of my reads/studies is Alan Dugan's *Poems Seven,* a Christmas gift from my father.

While I was growing up, our family often went on trips together, both because our parents wanted us to see a lot of the U.S., and also to experience nature through camping. We brought pets and friends. This helped me better appreciate poets like Robert Frost.

All our times together as a family included some kind of adventure and we had many warm and happy times. Sometimes just moving on the road would get boring and we would read aloud to stay entertained. Also, we would read aloud together at night around the campfire. By telling ghost stories, we hoped to spook each other into insomnia.

The camping trips started at a time after we'd moved into the 'big' house in Louisville's Audubon Park. When we'd grown too old for Mother's reading to us on the steps before bed, we still had our own books to read in our own beds, with our various pets—until, 'lights out' and 'quiet prayer.'

AS A CHILD

A WEEKEND MORNING OF CHILDHOOD

The birds of spring are singing outside the windows by my soft, cozy place of slumber. Early morning sun is seeping in through the white shades. Little, bony Curt climbs onto the untidy covers, cuddly and cute in his nightly attire. Lisa still sleeps soundly in the matching bed next to mine.

"Let's make a tent," whispers my tiny brother, as if in secrete and we do.

Together we pull the big, heavy bedspread over various chairs and begin gathering. At last, we fill the empty space inside with many stuffed animals surrounding the room, and with other toys lying about.

I, at least, am fully awake and hungry by the time this project is finished. Carefully, then, we tiptoe downstairs for my favorite breakfast of chocolate chip cookies. Curt, as playful conspirator, carries the forbidden meal into the sunroom where I turn on the Saturday morning cartoons.

In the easily created contentment of childhood, he and I curl up under a generous blanket to watch the simple entertainment. Eventually, overcome with the sugary energy of our loot, we begin to wrestle and giggle. We play with the curly, brown and floppy dog just settled at the end of our outfit.

Listlessly little Lisa shuffles in rubbing the sleep from her eyes. She slumps sluggishly down on top of the mound where Curt and I continue our roughhousing. She is soon roused out of her drowsiness and, as Lisa joins in, the room is warm with laughter.

AND AGAIN, ONE CHILD'S SATURDAY MORNING

Dad is downstairs having his breakfast. He's very cranky in the mornings and I am afraid of him then, so I and my cat wait at the top of the stairs. She for her breakfast and me for my cue that the downstairs is safe.

After eons I hear the outside kitchen door close and begin dragging the cat, big as me, down the steps. She's not a very friendly cat really, but she's mine, so I have to take care of her.

I put her in place on the kitchen desk and fill her bowl with tuna fish. The, I go to the cabinet for my own breakfast of Chips Ahoy, and head for the TV. set.

The sunroom is light with morning as I go to turn on the cartoons. I curl up under the big blanket on the couch to watch the elemental entertainment.

This blissful solitude doesn't last for long. I hear little Lisa coming down the stairs with the young Curt in tow. They're giggling and silly. They'll wake the somewhat elder Lee, who will then wander down, a bit more subdued and to herself.

Lisa and Curt roam into the sunroom for breakfast with me. It's the weekend! Glorious Saturday! We play and romp about until Mom emerges from her slumber and room to see what's up with her rather rambunctious offspring.

She is concerned. "Leslie, why don't you come into wake me up anymore?"

STAUNCH LESSONS

CENTRE COLLEGE AFFAIR

Books, mostly philosophical, line the walls of the old Victorian bedroom. This, in addition to the safari atmosphere created by zebra spread, old trunks, wine bottles and backgammon boards, serves to impress me beyond a point at which I am comfortable. The thought of the antique MG to which we will return for some "worldly" excursion, i.e., to the Danville Holiday Inn for brunch, is also dangerously intoxicating.

This is the reason that when he asks if I have a date to the Sigma Chi Valentine's dance, I answer honestly rather than tactfully. I will be going with one of his fraternity brothers. He is quick with the response that he too has made previous plans to attend with his "X."

At the dance, neither of us is much aware of the presence of our dates. He has attired his long, pale physique with a striking black tux. I wear a navy blue evening gown, cut low in the front and with a hood that hangs down the back. I bought the dress in hopes that it would attract his gaze by enhancing both my darker complexion and much smaller stature.

I sense his nearness intensely the entire evening. The feel of his eyes on me makes me proud. He teasingly places his top hat on my head and this small gesture of possession leaves me wondering.

The spring draws us closer, yet some very strong sense of uncertainty leaves me unable to reveal the intensity of my feelings for him. In an attempt to confuse him I date men who hold no interest for me. His jealousy is obvious. Still, his intentions remain a mystery.

At the end of the third trimester he graduates and leaves for work in Belgium. In the fall I return to school to continue my education.

LAST NIGHT

Again he leaves
without a word
and footsteps heard
into the hall
disappear

and the door closes.

LEAVE TAKING

He closes the door of the truck
and turns the key.

He backs out one last time.

He lights another cigarette
and slowly inhales the stale smoke.

CHANGES OF SEASONS IN PIECES OF THE CITY

CITY NIGHT

Only a siren screams into the hot hazy night,
then
the dark city seems stealthily silent.

The black red sky is haunted by a single star
and the glare of a yellow moon.

ACORNS IN AUGUST

Another magnificent storm last night.
Tremendous threats of light
          at the window
                    and thunder,
send the dog onto my bed.

Then, in the quiet of the morning
as I walk outside with him,
I notice, in the refuse of the angry weather,
          acorns on the fallen branches
          and, again, mushrooms growing in the yard.

Autumn is anxious to come.
It will bring welcome relief
from this summer's tormenting heat.

AUTUMN SUNDAY AT THE RIVER

In the cool early morning
the timeless river moves quietly on its way,
as old men in strategic fishing spots
carefully tend to their ancient task.

Small waves slap at the still solemn shore,
while water fowl fly about
in search of their simple sustenance.

WINTER NIGHT

Many stars shine brilliantly
against the black night
and rest quietly on bare branches
that reach solemnly for eternity.

WINTER WALK

Only a gentle shower of small ice
  disturbs the quiet.

Soft warm light from shining windows
  spills out into the evening solitude
  and old street lamps glow golden in the dusk.

  The tall crooked trees
  stand like ominous shadows
  reaching into a grey sky.

THE TRAUMA

WINTER'S COMING

Brown leaves litter
the frozen ground
like forgotten dreams
and the cold earth waits
in silent mourning.

Above,
many stars glow bright
with apprehension
against
a clear dark night.

BLEAK OMENS

The sky is shades of grey
and the naked trees
stand against it
like black skeletons.

They reach up
their bony fingers
for fragments of warmth
from the heavens.

STORMS

Autumn is coming in
with a constant thunder,
two nights this week
and one last.

The animals won't rest through it.
Their eyes light up like the sky.

These storms are so mad,
that sleep won't stay.
What anger awaits
the months to come?

DAD

Every night for over a week he slept in a chair,
beside her bed,
in the Open Heart Unit.
This man who was her husband of forty-five years.

Finally, when it was the consensus of her doctors and nurses
that she could be moved to the Transitional Care Unit,
he moved his things in with her.
There he had a cot.

On nights when she wasn't so bad, he'd let certain
of his children stay in his place.

Then Dad could go to the privacy of their home
and mourn for what was happening to their life.

He never stayed away long. Even though the nurses were angels
and he knew the family he had, that he could count on.

He knew his place and he knew where he wanted to be.
This man who was her husband of forty-five years.

When she left,
Dad was holding her hand
and had a chance to give her one last kiss,
which she will keep on her lips for all of eternity,
because she so dearly loved
This man who was her husband of forty-five years.

MOM

Mom's cousin, Delores, said of her
"Your mother was always my idol,
because she was so beautiful."

And she was beautiful.

That's why it was so hard to come home
after,
because everything in and around that house
that is beautiful
is her.

When our dear friend Donna Beals
came to visit last year with her son, Scott,
he commented to his mother, "What a gracious lady,
to make a pot of soup for us
even when she is so ill."

Mom, the lady of a thousand cookbooks.

But, she had recipes for your heart, as well
and those we will miss the most.

We kept telling her in the hospital,
so that she will never forget,
wherever her soul or spirit rest or wonder—
with God or with us—
"We love you, Mom. We love you."

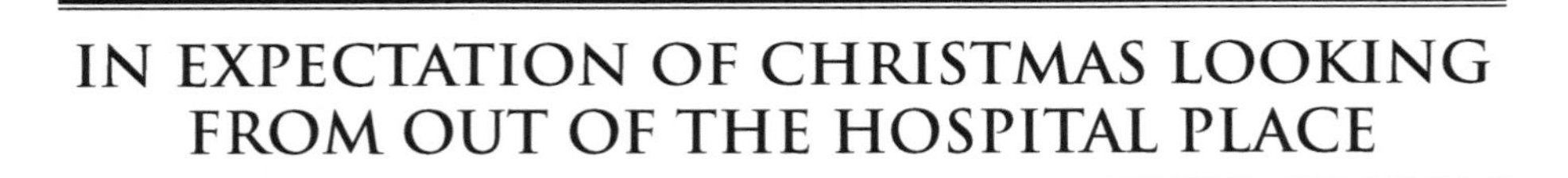

IN EXPECTATION OF CHRISTMAS LOOKING FROM OUT OF THE HOSPITAL PLACE

WINTER'S PROMISE

Outside the silent window glow,
        the purity of snowfall flows.
A soft and gentle silent know
        of why we're here
        and where we'll go.

AWAITING

Roof tops white with winter's kiss,
Sit silent in the grey dawn's mist.

As dark hands reach for Advent's light,
The Star of David yet in sight.

Outside the wind whisks cold the air,
It flies about like angels' hair.

ADVENT SUNDAY MORNING

A pale pink morning
leaves a light glow
on the ice
outside the window.

As the sun lifts
and brightens
the ice stays,
but slowly
the day
warms it
down.

This is an Advent Sunday
made for light
and right.

PREPARATION

Ice glistens up high on the church top,
like God's breath frozen.
Reflecting the bright pink dawn
of a new winter's day.

The church must be filled
with the happiness
of pious people
readying themselves
for Christ's coming.

CHRIST IS COMING

Early in the morning
when it is still out
and very dark,
all I see
are the colored lights
on the Christmas tree
outside my window,
and the large white star
on top
going to and fro.

It gives hope
for the season
and for what it will bring.

There are blessings here
for those of us
who can somehow
hold to faith.

OUTSIDE THE CHRISTMAS WINDOW

A pink, blue slated sky.
A grey colored day's beginning,
    but the Christmas tree lights shine
        ever so brightly
        in the dim.

A white star glows
    as the sky turns mauve.

Ice has stayed through the night.
Blue will bring warmth
    and the ice will fade away again.

Another day will pass
    with pinks, greys,
    and blues—
    even with some Christmas lights.
Then with the wait for tomorrow's beginning.

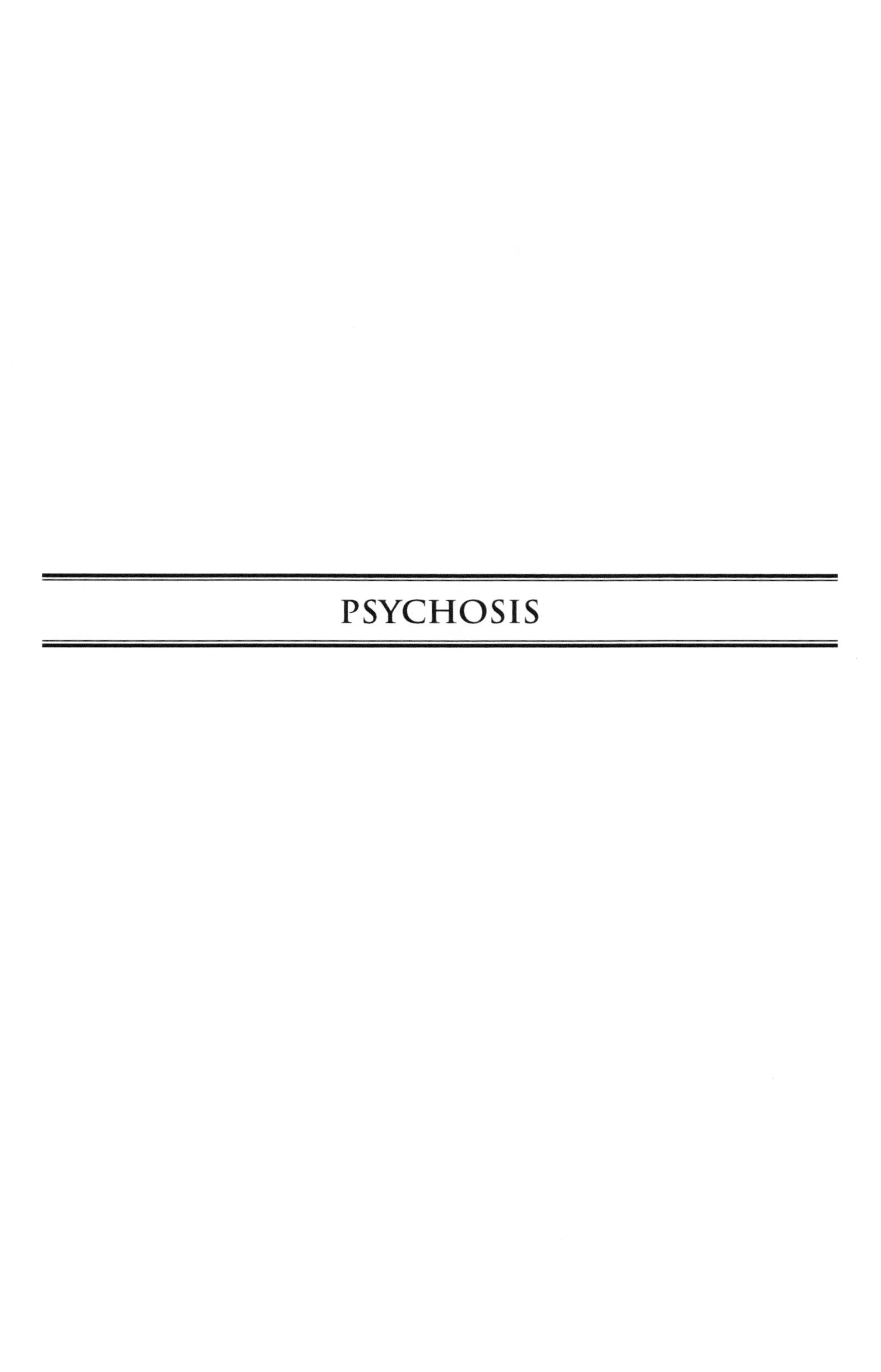

PSYCHOSIS

CONFUSION

This is a strange abode.
Weird sounds abound.
They come and go
like haunting spirits.

There are people here
who I cannot see.
They pass by my door.
Annoying presences.

If I leave,
they will follow.

I keep trying to find them,
but cannot.

UNDETECTED DOMINATION

I'm rarely ever left alone,
not allowed to eat,
told what to do
and what not to do,
day and night.

I must obey.
Something tells me I must,
so I do.

How awfully diligent, self-controlled
and frightened
I am.

LOOKING OUT FROM OTHER HOSPITAL SPACES

IN HERE

Outside the walls are concrete.
Rusted iron guards the windows.

Still, the sun is out.
It looks to be warm.

HOPE

No sun today—
just concrete
and iron
and rust—

And some green leaves
in a picture.

TODAY

The morning sky is still grey,
but the small stream
of traffic
has already started flowing
this early
at six a.m.

The city lights are dim
now
against the concrete buildings.

A close screech of brakes,
from the more imposing vehicles,
reminds me
that the peaceful dawn
is over.

DARK

No stars out,
just a few
city lights,
some on
the highway.

OUT

Morning light.
The day is mine.
Freedom!

Concrete, iron and rust

I will
leave
behind.

A GOODBYE TO DAD

HEALING HANDS OF OLD

If the kind of wisdom
that knows an unerring compassion
for all within his care
is tossed aside—
Who will do the real work, then?

If an understanding
that can be gained
only with age and experience
is thrown away—
Who will do the real work, then?

In a computer age
where profit matters more
than caring
and a bureaucrat can determine
who is allowed to survive—
Who will mind the real work, then?

When in truth,
it is the most tired eyes
that see the complete truth
and these are no longer cherished—
Who will do the real work, then?

NEW YORK

I remember going to Manhattan
and the boroughs,
when just a child,
to visit with
Grandfather Dame
and see the
New York World's Fair.

We were the barefooted
Kentucky children
playing on the
front porch stoop
in Queens.
We caused a stir.

(Later, on our visit to Syracuse,
Mom's best friend,
our Aunt Joy,
commented, with
a twinge of displeasure,
on the southern drawl
we were growing into.)

Most vividly I remember
getting lost,
from the family,
at the fair.
I was as frightened
as a child can be,
having no idea if
I would ever see
my family again.

As God might have it,
a lady both kind and wise
stopped to ask,
"Child, are you lost?"

She took me to a place
where children were taken
when they became separated
from their guardians.

Over a loudspeaker my father
was called for.
When I heard
his name
I was very gratified,
as always,
to hear my father
announced as 'Dr. Dame.'

I saw his face.
It was heaven sent.
He put me on his shoulders
and I felt
the most proud
little girl
at the fair.

I remember that ride atop
my father's shoulders
more than firework displays,
amusement park rides
or any of it.

Turns out,
there was a meaning
to that high, happy ride
on my father's shoulders
which none of the other
events held for me.

I think of my father
that way still,
as the one who will be there
even when I doubt.
He will come through the crowd.

OUR DOCTOR

I remember a man who
loved the winter,
most of all,
because he loved the snow.
I remember a man who
rode the sled
and gave turn to each of his children,
while they held fast, arms wrapped round him.
Then, he climbed with them back up the hill,
while teaching them just how to step.
I remember a man who built clever snowmen,
To teach his kids how to play in the snow.
He'd mold as with clay.
An artist this man was.
He was the one who built the fires,
trimmed and taught trimming of
the tree.
The Santa who brought home a few early
Christmas gifts,
for us, from his patients.
This is the man who
started out early,
and came home late from work,
to loud and often boisterous offspring.
He still takes medical calls
too often at night,
sometimes having to
leave home then, too.

This is the father who'd
cry for his dogs
that had died.
He feeds his
dogs, fish and birds
before leaving in the morning.
He keeps in his heart
a wife who passed on,
after almost forty-five years of marriage.
This is Dad.

THIS CHRISTMAS AT CHURCH, AFTER DAD

His head would fill with music.
His heart would burst with song.
His smile would fill the pew
as he'd greet you with a kiss.

Following the service,
at coffee,
his brain would brim with ideas.
he'd keep a conversation going
with such interest
as to give his company wait.

And now this Advent he's missing.
Messiah does not have its essence.
The pew is dim in his absence
and coffee is no longer a preferable choice.

THE MENTAL WARD—AGAIN

MONDAY, AUGUST 27, 2007

A Total Eclipse of the Moon

They've brought me here again,
People I do not know
and in an unkind way.

I have some clothes
And finally some peace.
The word is here—
other books.

I have a desk. The bed—that goes without sleep.
I have a sink and half bath.

The walls are a blue color.
A pretty picture
of Locust Grove
serves to sway
the utter degradation
of being here.

There is also a Norman Rockwell painting
in my hall.
The sun is up and in through the window.

I do not know what medicines
they will give me today.
That alone frightens me.

Where will I be
by the total eclipse of the moon?

MONDAY, AUGUST 27, 2007

Full Eclipse Of The Moon

Glowing shadowed globe
in a dusty blue sky.
Nine o'clock
the city is going to sleep.

An ambulance moves to the main
as a white van passes his side.
Garbage is put out for the day.
The professionals are going home to pray.

TUESDAY IN AUGUST

Following The Full Eclipse Of The Moon

How still the city
for a Tuesday afternoon,
hot in August.

So quiet
this morning
early a.m.

Not a person
on the street.

A bright blue sky,
white clouds included.

I hope sleep comes
a bit easier
tonight.

NIGHT AGAIN

The city is closing up.
        Cars are going home.
The street is quiet now.
        Sun is in.
Workers
        have said, "Good night."
Where have the rooftop birds gone?

THOUGHTS OF WORSHIP

AFTER THE SERVICE

The small church is quiet
        but altar candles are still warm,
        and the choir stalls are light with the resonance
        of today's hymns.

The pews are filled now only with the shadows of prayers:
        despair, gratitude, generosity, plea—
        all on wing to seek the Divinity
        that we worship here.

SAINT MARK'S

Candle light
at the
tall
church window

Makes a shadow
of the
path's tree branches,
still bare
with winter,
this
Lenten season.

THE CHURCH

Outside the candle lighted windows,
green leaves blow in a gentle wind.
The wooden cross hangs suspended
over the white linened altar,
freshly hallowed by newly colored flowers.
Close by a pianist plays
softly, reverently.
Quietly, the congregation gathers.

WINTER

COLD WINTER'S MORNING

Above the crunch of snow,
a half moon
is surrounded
by silver stars.

Bare black branches
reach up into a dark sky.

The glow of a street lamp
spreads through the open door
of a
warm
home.

FEBRUARY SNOW

Fragile fingers,
of bare trees,
reach hungrily
to the dusky sky.

From holy heavens
a soft snow
falls gently
to the
brown and frozen earth.

BRISK REST

A bright red spot
on the barren brown bush
awaits his discolored mate,
who is soon to arrive,
beneath the grey winter sky
that foretells of ominous weather
to come.

PALTRY THE DAY

A winter wind blows dry leaves
    into the smoky grey sky,
    while a slight freezing rain
    falls solemnly to the brown earth.

NIGHT WALK

The white church steeple glows
beneath three stars,
        in a night sky.

Black trees
        are yet cold
        with the winter's weather.

My footsteps are hushed,
        in the dark,
        and simple setting.

SPRING

GROWING UP

Long ago and far away,
the children gathered by the honeysuckle vine,
on a bright warm sunny day.

Mother told them where to look
and told them how to do.

Then the pretty little flower
became a honey dew.

SPRING

Sweet red breasted robin
looks up and winks at me.
He'd rather be on Barbara's fence
than in my flowered tree.

SPRING DAY

Little sparrow,
on the wing,
visits me
as if to sing.

He just looks in
and flies away.
We both have got
a busy day.

KNOWING

A funny feathered owl,
            on a closed up wooden fence.
It isn't even night.
A miracle

present.

MOM, DAD AND ME

I WISH I HAD

I wish I had
the little card table
she'd sit at
Christmas Eve.
She'd set it next to the Christmas tree.
Then, Mom would surround herself
with all of the necessary
gift wrap, ribbon, tape,
gift cards and gift bags.
She'd be dressed in her
pretty red, long, loose fitting
Christmas shift.
She'd set down a cup
of the eggnog she'd
made herself from scratch.
Then, Mom would get to work.
She'd work from early in the evening
until sometime in the a.m. hours.
On Christmas Day
the room was always a wonderland
created by our mother,
at her little card table.
It was put away now
and replaced by
all of the lovely wrapped gifts.

If she heard anything
about it,
she didn't hear nearly enough.
Certainly not:
"What beautiful wrapping Mom!"
"What a lovely bow Mother!"
"Oh, Mother, the room looks so incredible!"
"What an awful lot of time you must have spent!"
If she minded,
she never showed it
or said anything.
She was always very occupied,
off and on, Christmas morning
and all during Christmas Day
with the preparation of Christmas dinner.

Mom made all of the traditional dishes
from scratch
and mostly with very little help.
There would be the turkey
but, sometimes goose or duck
for Dad.
The dressing was sometimes chestnut
and sometimes oyster.
She made cranberry sauce, corn pudding,
and country style green beans.
Finally, also for Dad,
there was the plum pudding
with hard sauce.

I wish I had
even just a good few more
of her literally hundreds and hundreds
of cookbooks.
She collected them
from places where she traveled
with Dad and us.
She collected them
from places where she ate out
with Dad and us.
She collected them
from the shops
that she both visited
and regulared.
She said
that they were all
very necessary
because she used
even at least some
recipes out of
each and every one.
Mostly, she loved to cook
all kinds of different foods
and Dad loved to eat
all kinds of different foods.
There were the times
that she would look
very beleaguered and say,
"Oh, God! I've still got to go home
and cook dinner."

It was her duty
as a mother and wife
but, she said that
it was her most
favorite job
in the world.

I wish I had
her gardening tools.
She loved flowers,
all kinds
and she liked
to put their colors
around in order
to make them
look the most
beautiful to each other.
Much like she would
sew very like dresses
for we three girls,
as young children,
to make us look
the most becoming
to each other.

I wish I had
the last car
she ended up with,
the van.
That it were still in good condition
and running.
She must have spent
as much time
in a car,
out and about,
as she did at home.
Mostly, excited about
everywhere she went
and everything she did,
unless it came down to being an absolute job
like the weekly grocery store run.

God knows, what I really wish
I had is Mom.

A MAN OF HEALING

For a very long time
I remembered his hands
more than his face.

The hands that:
lay down the patient
on the examining table,
held the stethoscope to the heart,
felt for the wounded organ,
took that of a friend's.

Later, I remembered the face,
thank God.
In a dream.
He was smiling
and advising me on what to do.

If was the face that:
cried when his dogs died,
laughed with the family and friends
after telling often quite complicated jokes,
sang both church hymns
and Frank Sinatra in harmony,
kissed both 'good morning'
and 'good night'
to everyone in his family,
and finally, gave up the ghost
with a gentle smile on his lips.

THE PRAYER BENCH

Knowing takes a kind air,
a present of still peace.
The heart hears soft songs
of love's likeness.

Edwards Brothers Malloy
Oxnard, CA USA
November 20, 2014